Kate Peridot

Sama

Animal Gym School

BLOOMSBURY
CHILDREN'S BOOKS

LONDON OXFORD NEW YORK NEW DELHI SYDNEY

Most animals can **crawl**, **walk** or even **run** as soon as they are born. Human babies take a lot longer to learn how to move, but once children have found their feet, they are clever **copycats**. In fact, it's amazing what our bodies can do with a bit of **practice**!

So, who can inspire us to **move** in fun new ways?

Animals, of course.

Welcome to the Animal Gym School!

These animal friends are here to share why they move the way they do and to help you improve your **strength**, **speed** and **balance** by getting your whole body moving.

Are you ready to go? Let's meet the **animal gymnastics experts** ...

Do you have a favourite animal? How do they move?

Before moving, make sure the area is clear and there's a soft place to land. An adult should always be close by.

Walk like a bear

Brown bears are **curious creatures** who don't like to hurry. They **wander** through the forest, **sniffing** for juicy berries and bugs to eat.

Sometimes they **stand up tall** on their hind legs to see who's coming, then disappear into the forest before you can spot them.

1 Walk lazily on your **hands** and **feet** with your **knees** slightly bent.

Bottom high

Hands slightly turned in

2 Every so often, **stand up tall** to look around ... can you see another bear nearby?

Gallop like a zebra

When a zebra sees a lion, it **snorts** a warning to the herd. They **spring** into a **gallop** and off they go – **leaping** over logs and **zigzagging** this way and that.

Faster and *faster* the zebras **race** until they are safe again, out on the wide-open grassy plains.

Zebras have excellent eyesight and hearing for sensing danger, and are super-speedy runners.

1 **Step one foot forwards**. This will be your lead foot.

2 Quickly chase the **heel of your lead foot** with the **toes of your back foot** again and again.

Swap legs when the lead leg gets tired.

Galloping is a lot like skipping. You will land on your back foot first.

Hop like a kangaroo

Kangaroos **bounce** everywhere ...

BOING, BOING, BOING!

Their long legs are like **giant springs** and their tails help them to **balance**. They **hop** for hours across the outback desert in search of water and new grass to eat.

Baby joeys ride in their mums' pouches until they're big enough to keep up with the group.

1 **Stand** with your feet together and knees slightly bent. **Hold your hands up** in front of your chest like paws.

2 Hop forwards, making little hops, then **BIG hops**. Then jump to the left, and then to the right in a **zigzag** pattern.

How fast can you go?

Balance like a leopard

Who is that spying on the world below from the top of a tree? A leopard **walks** from branch to branch, perfectly **balanced**, searching for a comfy spot to rest.

Up high, he can **watch out** for prey, hide from lions and eat his dinner in peace.

Leopards use their strong legs and grippy claws to keep safe while balancing.

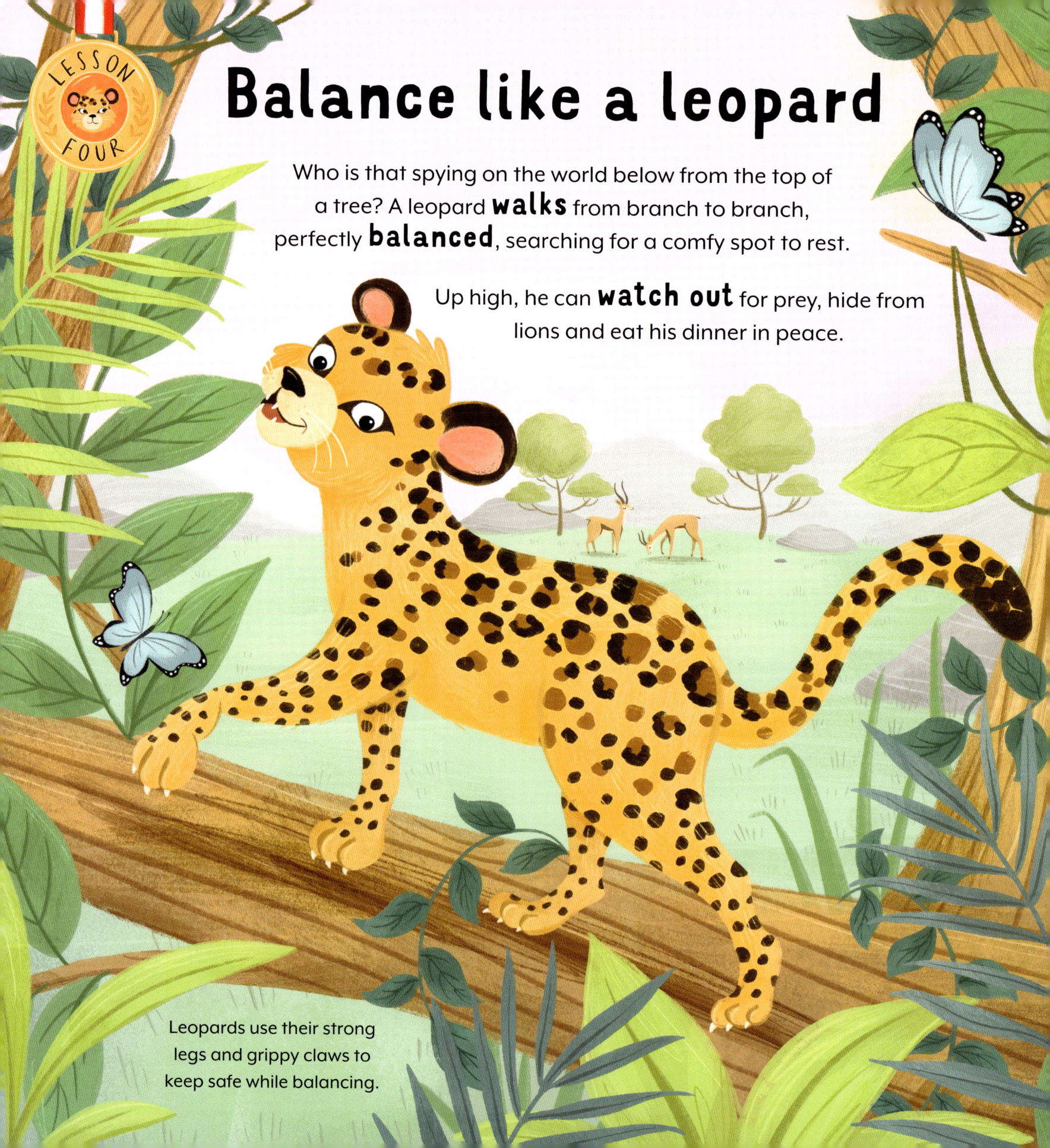

1 Step onto the end of a balance beam and **walk forwards**, placing **one foot in front of the other**.

Hold your arms out for balance.

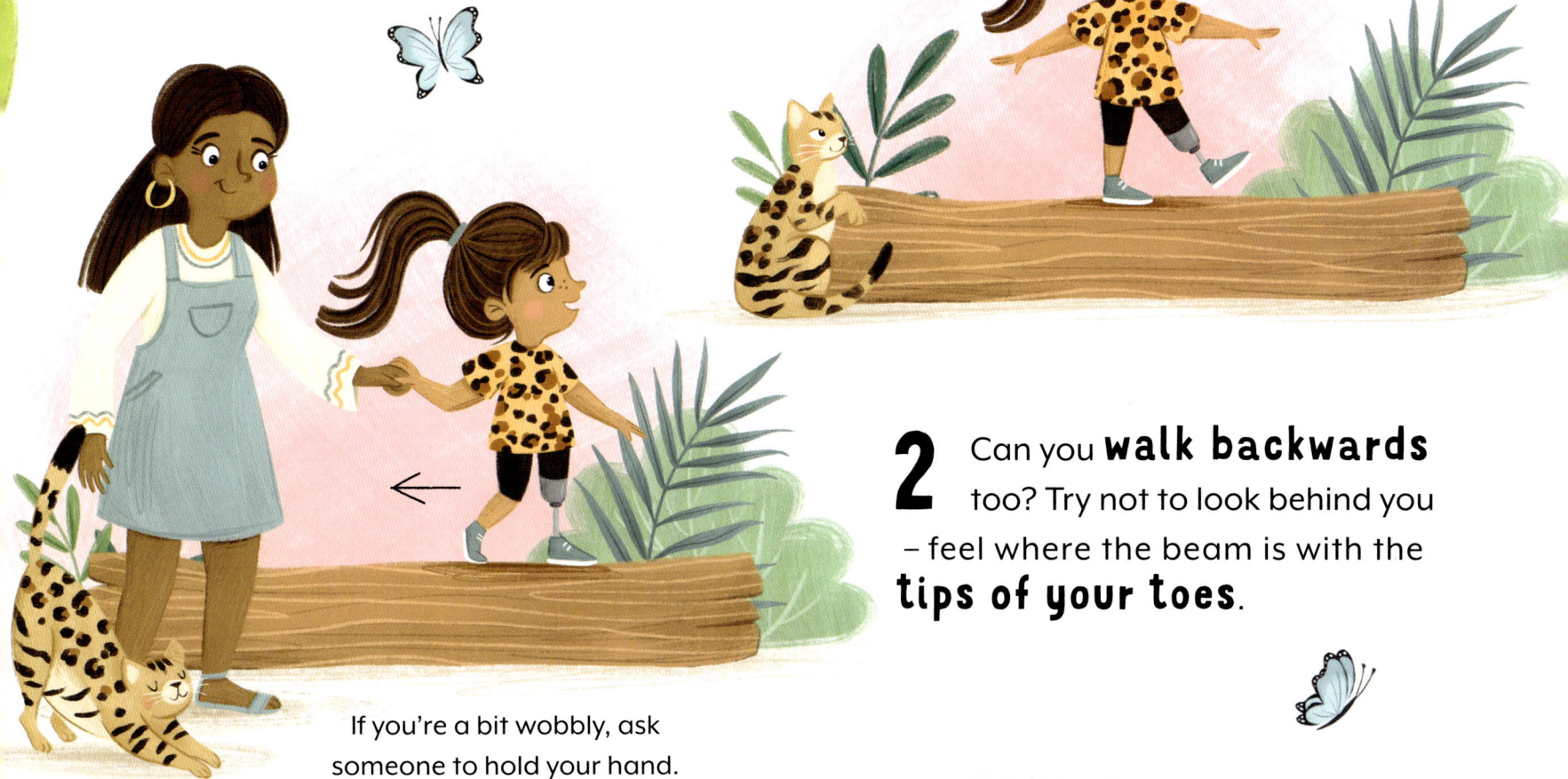

2 Can you **walk backwards** too? Try not to look behind you – feel where the beam is with the **tips of your toes**.

If you're a bit wobbly, ask someone to hold your hand.

3 Walk **forwards** and **backwards**, as graceful as a cat!

Scuttle like a crab

By day, crabs rest in rocky crevices and at night, they **scuttle sideways** in search of food. Crabs will munch on anything they can catch with their **snappy claws**.

But when a hungry seagull spies them ...

QUICK,

little crab, bury yourself in the sand!

1 Sit with your **knees up** and **feet in front of you** and snap your fingers together like crab claws. **SNAP, SNAP!**

2 Put your hands on the floor behind you and **lift your bottom up.**

3 **Raise your back** with your tummy facing upwards.

4 **Walk** on your **hands and feet**, going forwards and backwards.

Which way is easier?

Roll like an armadillo

Shhh! This armadillo is very shy and only comes out of her burrow at night to raid ant nests. Her body is covered in **armoured plates**.

When she's frightened, she **jumps** in the air, **tucks in** her feet, head and tail, and **SNAPS** into a ball.

Only the South American three-banded armadillo can curl into a ball.

1 **Squat** with your feet together, hands on the floor and **chin tucked** into your chest.

2 **Lift** your bottom and **lower** the back of your head onto the mat. Gently **push** from your feet ...

Back curved like a ball

3 ... and **ROLL!**

Can you stand straight up after you roll?

Handstand like a skunk

The spotted skunk sees a prowling coyote. To look bigger and scarier, the skunk **balances** on his front paws with his **tail high in the air**.

When the coyote doesn't leave, the skunk sprays a strong, **stinky musk** right in the coyote's face. *Phew!* That makes the coyote change his mind!

Skunks come out at night. Their black and white coat helps them to hide in moonlight shadows.

1 Hold your arms up straight and step into a **lunge**.

Put your weight on the front foot.

2 In one quick movement, **bend down** at the waist, put both hands flat on the ground and **kick your back leg upwards** ...

3 ... quickly followed by your **front leg**. Your legs should come together with your body in a **straight line**.

It takes practice. Start against a wall or ask an adult to catch your legs.

Tighten your tummy muscles.

Head down

4 Put one leg down at a time and return to the starting position.

Cartwheel like a spider

Uh oh! A wasp is chasing the golden wheel spider. The spider **flips** onto her side and **cartwheels down** the steep sand dunes of her desert home. She's so fast, the wasp can't keep up! Then she drops back on her feet and creeps away.

During the day, the spider hides in deep burrows. She weaves sticky webs to hold up the walls of her sandy home.

1 Hold your arms up straight and **step into a lunge**.

Toes pointed lightly outwards for balance

Weight on the front foot

2 Place your hands on the floor, one in front of the other in line with your front foot and raise **your back leg** upwards ...

3 ... in one quick movement **swing your legs up and over**, balancing your weight on one hand, then the other.

Try to straighten your legs!

4 Land one foot at a time.

5 Then stand with your **arms raised**. Ta-dah!

Climb like a sloth

A baby sloth learns to climb a tree in the Amazon jungle. He **grips** with his clawed feet and **reaches** up with one arm, then the other, *soooo* slowly! Sloths *never* hurry. When he's tired, he clings to his mum and she finds a safe spot high in the branches to sleep all day.

Three-toed sloths can turn their head almost all the way around.

1 **Reach up** and grip firmly onto the bar or rope.

2 **Climb** onto the frame by **pulling up** with your arms and **pushing off** with your feet.

3 Move your hands and feet up to find new places to grip onto the bar or rope.

Move one hand or foot at a time.

If you find a place to perch, keep holding on with **both** hands while you enjoy the view!

4 To get down, move backwards with your **feet first** and feel for safe hand and footholds.

Always **climb down slowly!**

Swing like a gibbon

The gibbon family sings with **HOOTS** and **HOWLS** as they swing through the rainforest treetops, graceful as acrobats. Gibbons' strong, **long** arms and **hook-shaped hands** grab branch after branch. Quick as a flash, they change direction when they spot their favourite fruit.

When on the ground, gibbons walk holding their long arms up, so they don't drag on the floor.

1 A **strong grip** is needed to swing. Practise by hanging from two bars. Pull up with one arm, then the other, and swing from side to side.

2 Once you feel strong enough, start at the beginning of the monkey bars. **Grab** the first bar with one hand and then swing out, bringing your hands together.

3 Grab the next bar and **keep swinging forwards**, one hand after the other.

If you can reach, swing from one bar to the next one without your hands meeting first.

4 Bend your knees to land safely when you drop to the ground.

Swing your legs forwards to help

Pose like a flamingo

The flamingo mum has flown a long way to find a shallow lake with lots of food to raise her chicks. When resting, the chicks copy the rest of the flock. They tuck in their wings and **stand on one foot**, holding up the other leg to keep warm.

Flamingos are born white or grey. A chemical in the algae they eat turns their feathers peachy pink!

Feel your shoulders stretching.

1 **Stand tall** and hold your hands together behind your back and pull **downwards**. Count to 10.

2 Then release your hands and **stand** on one leg, flamingo style!

3 Grasp your raised foot, pulling it towards your bottom. Count to 10 to stretch your leg and then swap sides.

Try not to wobble!

Stretch like a giraffe

Munch, munch. Only the giraffe with her **long legs** and **neck** can **reach** the leaves at the top of the tree. She doesn't have to share them with anyone.

Oops! She's dropped some leaves. Her neck isn't quite long enough to reach the ground so she must stand with legs slightly apart to eat them.

Giraffes don't often lie down to go to sleep. It's too difficult to get up again. They take lots of short naps standing up!

1 **Stand** with your legs straight, hip-width apart and **raise your arms** above your head. **Stretch the tips of your fingers** up to the sky.

2 **Bend** a bit to the left and then a bit to the right.

3 Come back to the centre and slowly **bend at the waist**. How far can you reach?

Repeat a few times.
Ah! It's lovely to streeeetch!

Laze like a lion

The lion family are hot and sleepy after a long night **stalking** antelope. When the sun comes up, they find a shady tree to laze under. The cubs play **pounce** until they're tired, and then **s t r e t c h** and **lie down** for a nap.

Lions are the only big cats to live in family groups, which are called prides.

1 **Get down** on all fours like a cat. Then **stretch your arms** forwards until your forehead rests on the floor but keep your bottom up!

2 Feel a lovely **stretch** through your back, shoulders and arms. **Hold** the position and count to 10.

3 Slowly return to all fours and then lie down and relax, any way you choose!

Practise all the animal movements!

Warm-up

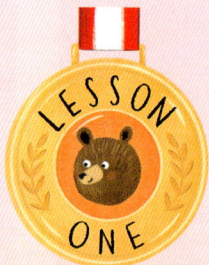

LESSON ONE
Walk like a bear

LESSON TWO
Gallop like a zebra

LESSON THREE
Hop like a kangaroo

Skilled

LESSON FOUR
Balance like a leopard

LESSON FIVE
Scuttle like a crab

LESSON SIX
Roll like an armadillo

Expert

LESSON SEVEN
Handstand like a skunk

LESSON EIGHT
Cartwheel like a spider

LESSON NINE
Climb like a sloth

LESSON TEN
Swing like a gibbon

Cool down

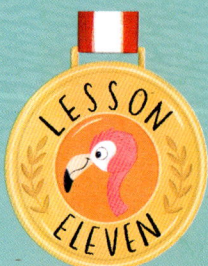

LESSON ELEVEN
Pose like a flamingo

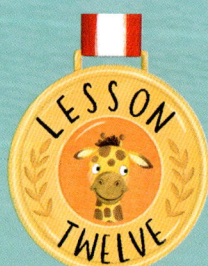

LESSON TWELVE
Stretch like a giraffe

LESSON THIRTEEN
Laze like a lion

Well done, you're an amazing mover!

Now, are you ready to move like a human?
Invent some moves and put your own routine together ...

Keep moving!

For Jess & Jack who stomp like elephants! – K.P.
For Team DLJ x – S.H.

BLOOMSBURY CHILDREN'S BOOKS
Bloomsbury Publishing Plc
50 Bedford Square, London, WC1B 3DP, UK
Bloomsbury Publishing Ireland Limited
29 Earlsfort Terrace, Dublin 2, D02 AY28, Ireland

BLOOMSBURY, BLOOMSBURY CHILDREN'S BOOKS and the Diana logo
are trademarks of Bloomsbury Publishing Plc

First published in Great Britain 2025 by Bloomsbury Publishing Plc

A catalogue record for this book is available from the British Library

ISBN: PB: 978-1-5266-5700-8; eBook: 978-1-5266-7411-1

2 4 6 8 10 9 7 5 3 1

Printed and bound in China by RR Donnelley, Dongguang City, Guangdong

FSC
www.fsc.org
MIX
Paper | Supporting
responsible forestry
FSC® C144853

To find out more about our authors and books visit
www.bloomsbury.com and sign up for our newsletters

For product safety related questions contact productsafety@bloomsbury.com